FABIANISM
AND
THE EMPIRE
A MANIFESTO
BY THE FABIAN SOCIETY

Elibron Classics
www.elibron.com

Elibron Classics series.

© 2005 Adamant Media Corporation.

ISBN 1-4021-0609-2 (paperback)
ISBN 1-4021-0608-4 (hardcover)

This Elibron Classics Replica Edition is an unabridged facsimile of the edition published in 1910 by Grant Richards, London.

Elibron and Elibron Classics are trademarks of Adamant Media Corporation. All rights reserved.

This book is an accurate reproduction of the original. Any marks, names, colophons, imprints, logos or other symbols or identifiers that appear on or in this book, except for those of Adamant Media Corporation and BookSurge, LLC, are used only for historical reference and accuracy and are not meant to designate origin or imply any sponsorship by or license from any third party.

FABIANISM AND THE EMPIRE

FABIANISM AND THE EMPIRE: A MANIFESTO BY THE FABIAN SOCIETY. EDITED BY BERNARD SHAW

GRANT RICHARDS, 9, HENRIETTA STREET, LONDON, W.C. 1900

CHISWICK PRESS : CHARLES WHITTINGHAM AND CO.
TOOKS COURT, CHANCERY LANE, LONDON.

EDITOR'S PREFACE.

As the word editor is not a term of precision, it is necessary to explain that it means, in this instance, only the draughtsman employed by the eight hundred members of the Fabian Society to produce their Election Manifesto. The Society is alive to the importance of making its utterances readable; and this can only be done by leaving the manner of their expression to a literary expert, and confining its dictation to the matter to be expressed.

Further, it will be understood that the greatest common measure of the opinions of eight hundred persons is not the same thing as the opinion of every individual member, and that on certain points a wholly dissentient minority has been small enough to submit to being voted down. For example, some members regard the South African expedition as a foreseen and deliberate act on the part of the Government; and of these, some consider it a political crime, and others a justifiable stroke of Imperial Statesmanship. Again, on the point of Army Reform, many members disapprove so strongly of war that they desire it to be understood that they endorse the pages which follow on that subject only as a Tolstoyan opponent of our criminal system might nevertheless provisionally advocate prison reform, or as a vegetarian might advocate municipal abattoirs. There are Fabian teetotalers, too, who refuse to say anything more for the municipal public house than to admit, doubtfully and reluctantly, that it is a more controllable evil than a brewer's tied house, and will not go even so far as that without an explicit affirmation that a more excellent way is not to have drinkshops of any sort. All reservations made, however, it may be taken that what is said in this Manifesto is what the great majority of the members of the Fabian Society desire to have said at the present moment.

It must not be inferred from the restriction of the Manifesto to the general lines of the reforms advocated that these have been but superficially considered. Our allusion to the Drink Question, for instance, clearly does not exhaust it, since a considerable interval of regulation of private enterprise lies between us and complete municipaliza-

tion. But the tracts prepared by Mr. Edward Pease, and already issued by the Society, supply the lacking proposals. Again, the inevitableness of the Minimum Wage, which is no mere theoretic remedy, but the irresistible conclusion from a century of labor organization, has come out in the course of a unique investigation, the most elaborate and severe yet undertaken by individual Fabians, by Mr. & Mrs. Sidney Webb. It is recorded in their volumes entitled "The History of Trade Unionism" and "Industrial Democracy." The suggestion as to the provision of a Militia by raising the half-time age was first mooted by them in a letter to The Times last year. The important proposals as to the consular service are the outcome of a series of discussions initiated by Mr. S. G. Hobson, who was the first Fabian to see the value, as an illustration of the need for State organization of foreign trade, of the contrast between the imbecility and paralysis of English commercial diplomacy in the valley of the Yang-tse, and the victorious alertness and efficiency of Russia. As to Municipal Trading, those who are not yet alive to the fact that we are in the throes of a struggle—quite as important as the South African one—between the new local *authorities, representing the citizenship of England, and the company promoters, for the control of our common life industries, will find in the Fabian tract on " The Economics of Direct Employment," and that on " The Growth of Monopoly " by Mr. H. W. Macrosty, a mass of facts which cannot be detailed in an Election Manifesto. The elector who votes in ignorance of these facts will vote on assumptions which, though they are unfortunately still the prevalent assumptions of our educated classes, have long ceased to have any relation to contemporary reality.*

For many valuable amendments and certain chastening criticisms, I am indebted to several members of the Society; but those named above, with Mr. Gilbert Slater, have contributed as well as criticised.

One of the reasons for issuing this Manifesto in the form of a shilling book is that the custom of the Society, which is to sell for a penny a quantity of literary matter and political and statistical information which could not be commercially produced and sold for less than half-a-crown, has resulted in an undue specialization of its market. The richer classes in England read nothing but what their booksellers sell; and booksellers cannot afford to sell penny pamphlets. It is one of the oddities of our competitive system that, out of the multitude of useful things that are sold for a penny, the millionaire can only obtain the penny stamp and the penny newspaper: if he wants the penny Fabian Tract he must either join one of the political or social organizations by which such wares are distributed (and their articles of faith are seldom such as a conscientious millionaire can subscribe), or else the Society must come to his rescue by charging him at least a shilling. It does so in this instance with many apologies for the smallness of the sum, which is, nevertheless, an exclusive one—how exclusive the reader will best appreciate after a reference to our " Facts for Socialists," facts which unfortunately remain facts from edition to edition, in spite of our sixteen years' struggle to awaken social compunction concerning them.

G. B. S.

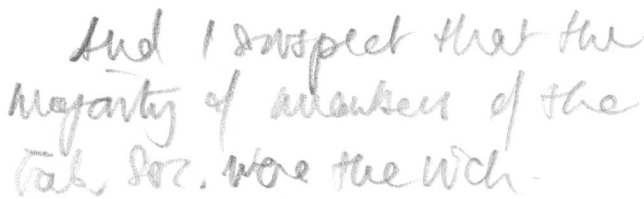

CONTENTS.

PART I. FABIANISM AND THE EMPIRE.

	PAGE
INTRODUCTORY	1
FOREIGN TRADE	7
IMPERIAL POLICY	13
INDIA	17
SOUTH AFRICA: The Gold of the Rand	22
The Settlement	31
ARMY REFORM	38
Shall we have Conscription?	39
The War Office	43
CHINA	44
Free Trade	50
"Panem et Circenses"	52

PART II. HOME AFFAIRS.

HOME AFFAIRS	59
The Working Classes	60
Labor Policy	62
A Minimum Wage for Labor	64
THE HOUSING QUESTION	68
MUNICIPAL TRADING	72
THE DRINK QUESTION	80
The Public House	81
EDUCATION	85
The Press	91
THE MORAL OF IT ALL	93

PART I
FABIANISM AND THE EMPIRE

FABIANISM AND THE EMPIRE.

INTRODUCTORY.

THE forthcoming General Election will turn, we are told, mainly on the popularity of Imperialism. If this be so, it is important that voters should make up their minds what Imperialism means. If it is a mere catchword vaguely denoting our insular self-conceit, then its victory at a General Election would be a grave symptom of national infatuation. But if it means a well-considered policy to be pursued by a Commonwealth of the communities flying the British flag, then it is as worthy and as weighty an issue as an election could turn on. Only, in that case, we must ask for a clear statement of the questions that have been considered, and the solutions proposed for them.

So far, no such statement has been made. The pressure of war, far from changing our parliamentarians into statesmen, has only freshened the stale levities of partisanship by an outbreak of boyish excitement and an occasional flush of indignation that is, for once, not a pretence to be dropped the moment the speaker leaves the platform. Thus, when opponents of the Government's policy have had their windows broken, the leader of the House of Commons has naïvely blurted out the feeling of the Government that it served them right. The Colonial Secretary has publicly threatened France with war because the tone of some of the French comic papers is disrespectful to the British Empire. This was shortly after Punch had caricatured the French nation and Major Marchand as an organ-grinder with a monkey. All this may be natural enough; but it is not Imperial statesmanship. As to the Opposition, it is divided into three sections. Two of them are anxious to shew that they agree with the Government in everything except their desire to have a turn in office and the selection of the next Prime Minister. The third, though its intellectual honesty stands out well in the general parliamentary dearth of that quality, still clings to the fixed-frontier ideals of individualist republicanism, non-interference, and nationalism, long since demonstrated both by experience and theory to be inapplicable to our present situation. It is possible to respect the tenacity and courage of these sturdy gentlemen, just as it is possible to respect the tenacity and courage of President Kruger. But it is not possible to conduct the British Empire, or even, as we have seen, a little African republic, on their principles.

The problem before us is how the world can be ordered by Great Powers of practically international extent, arrived at a degree of internal industrial and political development far beyond the primitive political economy of the founders of the United States and the Anti-Corn Law League. The partition of the greater part of the globe among such Powers is, as a matter of fact that must be faced, approvingly or deploringly, now only a question of time; and whether England is to be the centre and nucleus of one of those Great Powers of the future, or to be cast off by its colonies, ousted from its provinces, and reduced to its old island status, will depend on the ability with which the Empire is governed as a whole, and the freedom of its Governments and its officials from complicity in private financial interests and from the passions of the newspaper correspondents who describe our enemies as "beasts." And as there is no evidence, so far, that the Houses of Parliament, as at present manned, fulfil these conditions, or that the Press is disposed to criticize them for not fulfilling them, the present probabilities point, not to English success on the great international plane of modern politics, but to disruption of the Empire from within by Declarations of Independence from disgusted and exasperated colonists, and, as to these islands, to a chronic militarist panic of foreign invasion, mitigated only by the hope that the other Powers may be as ignorantly and lazily governed as we are, and that in the last extremity perhaps America would come to our rescue. The recent vogue of militarism, which flourishes only in terrified nations, and the prevalence of bluster of the "who's afraid?" kind in the Press, are seriously disquieting social symptoms; though it remains to be proved by a General Election how far they have affected the nerves of the electorate.

No election, unfortunately, can be very reassuring under existing circumstances. The nation makes no serious attempt to democratize its Government, because its masses are still in so deplorable a condition that democracy, in the popular sense of government by the masses, is clearly contrary to common sense. Our only aristocracy is a hereditary aristocracy, which is an absurdity in modern society, where distinctions of caste are completely broken down by money. The hereditary aristocracy can stand in the way of a genuine aristocracy of capacity; but it is unable to defend its posts against the hustling of ambitious and successful representatives of commerce. The result is that our constitution, whatever it may be nominally, is in fact a plutocracy. The central Government is in the hands of two official cliques equally bankrupt in modern political science, supported in Parliament by the votes of a number of gentlemen who, having no political ideas, though plenty of commercial ones, have bought their seats as much as they have bought their horses and their private houses. Almost all of them have been enabled to effect this purchase by personal and class interests which are coming more and more into direct competitive conflict with the interests of English citizenship as represented by the new local authorities. Most of them depend on the votes of the working class, whose part in the political history of the last ten years has been a steady policy of maintaining a rich class for the sake of getting employment from it either directly or through the huge class of shopkeepers who regard rich customers as their natural prey. Our concern in this Manifesto is not specially for the wage-earning class, which is taking its own course and reaping only what it has sown, but for the effective social organization of the whole Empire, and its rescue from the strife of classes and private interests.

FOREIGN TRADE.

THE first step to be taken abroad, and one without which our trade can never pass through the doors our armies have battered down and kept open for cleverer races (the Jews) and better organized nations (the Germans), is a reorganization of our consular service. We have an Imperial Institute at South Kensington, where it is not the slightest use, except perhaps as a towering monument of an exceptionally silly job. We want an Imperial Institute at every important port or inland trade centre, and at every likely-to-be-important port or centre, with which we trade. At that Imperial Institute the British trader should find ready for him an Exchange for the exhibition of samples of his products, a staff of responsible interpreters, and a consulate of experienced men, not wasting their time in writing reports for home which few people read and nobody attends to, but making it their business, as experts, to catch and advise the British trader until he, too, becomes an expert.

Also to see that the speculator in damaged cargoes and adulterated goods shall do his cheating outside the Institute with interpreters and agents picked up at the street corner; so that the British Commonwealth shall not be discredited by them, and the native buyer shall learn that our old familiar friend, the independent Briton who scorns grandmotherly government, and will not be interfered with by Jacks in office, has probably the same reason for objecting to the consul as a pickpocket has for objecting to a magistrate. The consulate could itself act as broker, if necessary, and have a revenue from commissions, of which, however, the salaries of its officials should be strictly independent. When the time comes for our foreign trade to outgrow private enterprise, and be carried on by an industrial British fleet instead of by lines of commercial privateers, such a developed consulate will furnish the administrative machinery for the change.

In the meantime a reorganized consulate can do us good service incidentally by representing the interests of the Commonwealth as against the private financial interests of the rings into whose hands our foreign trade at present tends to fall. These rings have an appalling power of dragging us into wars by the simple process of attending to their business whilst we are neglecting ours. In doing so they are only doing their duty to their shareholders. If our Governments neglect their duty to *their* shareholders (that is, to the citizens of the Commonwealth), it is idle to blame " Capitalism " for the results. None the less is it true that a ring can get at the Press, not because the Press is corrupt, but because it is ignorant. The Press can get at the Government for exactly the same reason. Nobody supposes, for instance, that a trading ring and its financiers can walk into The Times office, and pay the editor and his staff a round sum of money for working up a few common grievances into a war fever. But The Times will do it without being paid, from pure ignorance and insular pugnacity. And our Ministers, taking their information and their ideas from The Times and the papers of which The Times is a type, will send out armed expeditions under the impression that they are defending the Empire and glorifying the flag, when they are, as everyone behind the scenes can see, being used by speculators as a ferret is used by a poacher. This danger will beset us until we have in every foreign market an organ of commercially disinterested industrial intelligence. A developed consulate would be such an organ; and until we have it private interests will be able to make wars at our expense, and with our armies, by simply prompting the pugnacity which distinguishes us. This pugnacity is not, as we are apt to imagine, an effect of our courage. The plain truth is that as we are a nation of civilians, exempt from compulsory military service, with no home experience of the horrors of war, and very rich into the bargain, war means nothing to us but romantic accounts in the newspapers of what is happening abroad, ending in a few pence more on the income tax. If war meant to us the bombardment of English towns and the laying waste of English counties, all the millionaires in Europe would not be able to persuade us to risk a skirmish to remedy a grievance at the Antipodes.

Any person who thinks this application of Socialism to foreign trade through the consular system impossible, also thinks the survival of his country in the age of the Powers impossible. No German thinks it impossible. If he has not already achieved it, he intends to; and if the German can do in social organization what the Englishman cannot do, the most patriotic course for our Chambers of Commerce will finally be to beg the German Emperor to annex the British Isles after our armies have cleared the way for Germans in Asia, Africa, and wherever else the markets were fortified against them. American traders already sell their exports in the Far East by a joint permanent exhibition in Tokio. As to the Russians, the opening of the Siberian railway has revealed exploits of industrial diplomacy on their part which fill English travellers with a dismayed sense of our wasted opportunities. We have plenty of administrative machinery to begin with: first, the commercial attachés of the Diplomatic Corps, who have done good service in Berlin and Paris; second, the Consular Service; third, the Colonial Office, an organization capable, as Mr. Chamberlain well knows, of enormous development. Nothing is more depressing than to compare the use we make of them all with the use we might make of them if only we would take our public business seriously.

An easier, weaker, lazier and hopelessly ineffectual way to deal with foreign competition is to impose duties on imports. This course is suggested, naturally enough, by the people who would make money by it at the expense of the rest of the consumer. Its adoption would stamp us as a flock of political gulls. But when once the feeling that "something must be done" seizes us, we will be gulled sooner than do nothing. Mere old-fashioned Free Trade talk will have no effect on a generation which has not been educated in Manchester economics. Nothing but a positive alternative policy will save us from floundering into reaction; and there is no practicable alternative except bringing the power, the information, and the organization of the Empire to the help of the enterprise of the individual trader. We allowed the McKinley tariff to cause great distress in South Wales for some years by bringing a flourishing industry (the tin plate) to a standstill for want of new markets to which a properly organized consulate could have guided it. Our notion of encouraging industry at that time was to compel importers to mark their goods with the country of origin. As a result, articles marked "Made in Germany" now take the same precedence in our retail shops as hall-marked silver.

IMPERIAL POLICY.

THE best chance for Khaki at this election is not its own popularity, but the absence of any alternative. The Opposition front bench, having no ideas and no program (any more than the Government), will fall back on recrimination about irrevocable bygones in South Africa, instead of accepting the situation which has been created, rightly or wrongly, and facing it. Whether the electorate shares President Kruger's political ideas, or believes them to be as obsolete as his theology, it probably suspects that if the Government had been as earnest in its efforts to stave off war as in its efforts to stave off Old Age Pensions there would have been no war. But the electorate does not believe, and has not the slightest reason to believe, that if the Opposition had been in power, it would have been a whit less capitalist-ridden than the Government. All Governments are capitalist-ridden, and will continue to be so until Socialism builds up the British State into something worthy of a sacrifice of private commercial interests by public men. Consequently, if the Liberal Pot tries to get into power by calling the Conservative Kettle black, it will fail; for, if the choice is to be between parties instead of between programs, the Conservative party is greatly to be preferred, since it can get larger measures of reform through the House of Lords than the Liberal party can; and the most active reformers have reason to prefer the affable frankness of the Conservative Minister who laughs at his own ignorance and is willing to be coached through his Bills, to the unteachable Liberal who feels bound by the Cobdenite tradition to affect the doctrinaire in political science and economics without genuine knowledge of either.

What is needed now is a definite constitutional policy to be pursued by the Empire towards its provinces. The real danger against which such a policy must be directed is not the danger of attack on the Empire from without, but of mismanagement and disruption from within. The British Empire, wisely governed, is invincible. The British Empire, handled as we handled Ireland and the American colonies, and as we may handle South Africa if we are not careful, will fall to pieces without the firing of a foreign shot.

The primary conditions of Imperial stability are not the same throughout the Empire. The democratic institutions that mean freedom in Australasia and Canada would mean slavery in India and the Soudan. We are no longer a Commonwealth of white men and baptized Christians: the vast majority of our fellow-subjects are black, brown, or yellow; and their creed is Mahometan, Buddhist, or Hindoo. We forbid the sale of the Bible in Khartoum, and punish British subjects in India for blasphemy against Vishnu. We rule these vast areas and populations by a bureaucracy as undemocratic as that of Russia. And if we substituted for that bureaucracy local self-government by the white traders, we should get black slavery, and, in some places, frank black extermination, as we have had in the "back blocks" of Australia. As for parliamentary institutions for native races, that dream has been disposed of by the American experiments after the Civil War. They are as useless to them as a dynamo to a Caribbean. We thus have two Imperial policies : a democratic policy for provinces in which the white colonists are in a large majority, and a bureaucratic policy where the majority consists of colored natives. Consequently the Empire cannot be governed either on Liberal or Conservative, democratic or aristocratic principles exclusively; and cannot be governed on Church of England or Nonconformist principles at all. An Imperial issue between these parties and creeds is necessarily a false issue.

So far, the broad divisions seem simple and well marked. But it happens that in the two provinces of the Empire which have just been visited by the most terrible of calamities—war, plague, and famine—neither method of government can be applied in its integrity.

INDIA.

TAKE the case of India, famine-stricken and plague-stricken. At present we govern India despotically and bureaucratically, treating the native as a child who must be governed for his own good. This is the kind of government that really deserves the epithet grandmotherly. Unfortunately, it has hitherto been criticised in our Parliament on home-made principles, the remedy proposed being to confer a parliamentary constitution on the native population. Without raising the question whether Indian subtlety understands parliamentary institutions too well or does not understand them at all, it is certain that they are, for many reasons, impracticable in India. But that is no reason for placing thousands of miles between the capable, educated Indian and the examinations for the Indian Civil Service,[1] and maintaining it so as to provide lucrative posts for Englishmen whose pensions

[1] The question of the worthlessness of our present examinations as a test for Indian capacity is dealt with further on under the heading of Education.

add cruelly to the drain of rupees from a very poor country to a very rich one. For India, therefore, we need:

I. An extension of the opportunities of Western "secondary education" for natives capable of it.

II. A considerable further Indianization of the higher grades of the Civil Service.

III. Multiplication of the provincial councils with limited powers under the guidance of the British Raj.

IV. A wise development of the germs of self-government existent in the village councils.

These, however, are merely reforms of political machinery. With the really horrible responsibility of the famines upon us, we cannot be satisfied with the official optimism which is content with a demonstration that India would be worse off without our administration. The same kind of optimism, leaning on idle literary contrasts of " the nineteenth century " with " the dark ages," shielded the degradation of our manufacturing and mining population by the industrial revolution in England, and held back Factory legislation for half a century. To tell us that there is no village problem in

India; that there is no manufacturing-district problem in India ; that there is no excessive taxation in India ; that village communism has decayed through its own rottenness, and not through Anglo-Indian ignorance of its nature and value; that the financial transactions between Great Britain and India are perfectly equitable; that, in short, the famines, the conditions of labor in the ginning mills, the poverty and hopelessness, are "the act of God," mitigable only by the vigilance of Lord George Hamilton, is to tax our patience too far. Such official apologetics can reassure no sensible citizen until we obtain some reasonably credible information through:

A. An investigation of the social causes of Indian famines as distinct from the meteorological causes.

B. An investigation of the way in which the industrial revolution now proceeding is affecting the standard of life of the natives.

Can it be doubted that the conclusions from such investigations would create an Indian industrial program, and add considerably to the Indian political program? And does anyone pretend that we already have the information such investigations would supply, or that our ignorance is doing India no harm?

In the meantime a more sympathetic attitude towards the aspirations, if not towards the precise program, of the Indian Congress, and a more courageous toleration of the native Press, may safely be recommended.

These changes cannot be brought about until we cease to sympathize with the strong caste feeling of the European, both official and merchant. That it exists, and that it has influenced for the worse the conduct of some of the Western Powers towards Japan in the Chinese crisis, is plain enough. Now an Indian is a man; and to be treated as "half devil, half child" is intolerable to every man, white or brown. Yet this attitude on the part of the ruling white aristocracy of India daily finds expression in unconscious contumely and sometimes in acts which are open outrages. The Indians live in an atmosphere of conquest; and to fight against an atmosphere is a task of such infinite difficulty that it makes them despair of all constitutional efforts to emancipate themselves.

It is important that Indian reforms should

be taken in hand promptly, if only because of their importance as Imperial experiments. For we shall find in Africa as well as in Asia that the races we have to govern no more consist exclusively of ignorant and helpless tribesmen, capable of nothing but pure tutelage, than our own population consists exclusively of ignorant and helpless agricultural laborers. And if we persist in the lazy policy of treating them like children, and adducing their submission as a proof that they are incapable of a share in government, until they rebel (meanwhile training regiments of them, be it remembered, in the use of modern weapons), then, after a long period of ill-will, during which they will be a menace to the Empire instead of a buttress, they *will* rebel; and their rebellion will prove our incapacity for governing, not theirs for being governed. In fact, our first duty to our subjects is to make them as independent of our guidance, and consequently as appreciative of our partnership, as possible.

SOUTH AFRICA.

THE GOLD OF THE RAND.

IN South Africa—and Imperial policy at the coming election will mean South Africa—the problem is still more complicated than in India; for in it neither democracy nor bureaucracy will serve alone, however modified. We are confronted there with colonies demanding democratic institutions in the midst of native races who must be protected despotically by the Empire or abandoned to slavery and extermination. And it is the Conservative party which has gone to war professedly on behalf of democracy; whilst the anti-Imperialist Liberals have the appearance of supporting the Boer oligarchy against it. What has really happened, however, is that a troublesome and poor territory, which the Empire cast off into the hands of a little community of farmer emigrants, has unexpectedly turned out to be a gold-reef; and the Empire, accordingly, takes it back again from the farmers. If the Empire were a piece of private property belonging to England (as most Englishmen think), and the Transvaal a farm privately owned by President Kruger (as the President explicitly affirmed without contradiction from Sir Alfred Milner at the Bloemfontein Conference), the transaction would be mere brigandage. And it may be conceded that to citizens and statesmen who are dominated by the morality of private property, the war must be demoralizing if they are on the side of the Empire, and shocking if they are on the side of the farmers. But it is impossible for a great Commonwealth to be bound by any such individualist superstition. However ignorantly its politicians may argue about it, reviling one another from the one side as brigands, and defending themselves from the other with quibbles from waste-paper treaties and childish slanders against a brave enemy, the fact remains that a Great Power, consciously or unconsciously, must govern in the interests of civilization as a whole; and it is not to those interests that such mighty forces as gold-fields, and the formidable armaments that can be built upon them, should be wielded irresponsibly by small communities of frontiersmen.

Theoretically, they should be internationalized, not British-Imperialized; but until the Federation of the World becomes an accomplished fact, we must accept the most responsible Imperial federations available as a substitute for it. This is the best answer, for the purpose of excusing the war, to President Kruger's statement at Bloemfontein that, in demanding the franchise for the Outlanders, we were asking him to give the title-deeds of "his" land to the laborers on it. Sir Alfred Milner had no reply at all, because, not being a Socialist, he quite agreed with the President's fundamental position, and so had to argue in the manner of the wolf with the lamb.

Khaki enthusiasts in search of an excuse for a war which they have supported in pure pugnacity will probably embrace this view of the situation, and pretend that they have held it all along. We must, however, dash the cup of salvation from their lips by pointing out that there has not yet been the slightest suggestion from the Government that the expedition to South Africa will have any other effect than to hand the gold-reef over absolutely to the cosmopolitan capitalists who formerly held it subject to the royalties which President Kruger and the Volksraad very properly exacted from them. We never dreamt of the importance to civilization of our taking back the gold-reef. We did not intend to take it back. Lord Salisbury, at the Mansion House, rashly repudiated any such intention. It is even contended by those who sympathize with the Boers that the capture of the gold-reef for the capitalists was the real purpose of the expedition. But such a view flatters the intelligence of the Government at the expense of its honesty. The Government never for a moment meant fighting, any more than the nation did. What happened was that The Times and certain other influential papers, too dependent on the fashionable classes to venture to agitate about home grievances, began to bluster for reforms in the Transvaal. It was quite evident to the Government and everyone else that this bluster had been instigated, and was being encouraged, by the financial interests represented by Mr. Cecil Rhodes, who, having given up as impracticable his original project of "cutting the painter" and founding an Afrikander United States, had fallen back on the next alternative: that of consolidating the Rand with the South African Province of the British Empire. Still, this did not affect the merits of the case. Mr. Rhodes and his friends had every right to agitate for the redress of the Outlanders' grievances, and to enlist British Government pressure on their side if they could; and the Government and the nation acted naturally and patriotically in sympathizing with the Outlanders, who were mostly our countrymen. But the grievances alleged, though some of them were real enough, were ludicrously unimportant in comparison with our cognate home grievances. Nobody in his senses would have contemplated a war on their account. A crusade against Russia on behalf of Finland, or against Turkey on behalf of Armenia, would have been by comparison a sane enterprise. However, when a first-rate European power is dealing with a tiny frontier State, a good deal may be done by a threat of force—to put it bluntly, by bullying. Accordingly, we proceeded to bully, never doubting for a moment that President Kruger must succumb when he was convinced that we were determined to stand no nonsense. By rallying to the encouragements of The Times, and keeping a stiff upper lip, we succeeded in so convincing him; and, to our intense astonishment, the result was that he suddenly produced a formidable armament of the effectiveness of which we had no suspicion; invaded our territories; and in a moment plunged us into a war which we had never really meant to undertake, for which we were quite unprepared, and on the issue of which our entire South African province was now staked, since it was evident that, if we were beaten, the victorious Boers would be forced, whether they desired it or not, to make their work sure by uniting South Africa in an independent Afrikander Federation. What followed is fresh in the memory of the electorate. Defeat after defeat, battalions captured, garrisons besieged, Europe delightedly cheering on the tiny but plucky combatant who was thrashing us, and The Times, ridiculous to the last, calling on the world to admire the fortitude and self-control with which the English nation bore humiliation and disaster without guillotining the Cabinet in the manner of mere foreigners.

Of course this state of things did not continue. The Government had got the nation into an appalling mess; but when once it was brought to its senses by President Kruger's cannon, it called up our huge reserves of men and energy; the excited nation responded; and the Boers were overwhelmed by main force, and their territory annexed. That is the story up to the present moment. It is not a story of ministerial corruption and conspiracy, as the extreme Opposition papers maintain. The suspicion that Mr. Chamberlain conspired with Mr. Rhodes to annex the Transvaal is no doubt one for which he has himself and the abrupt suppression of the Jameson Raid inquiry to thank; but the notion that Lord Salisbury and Mr. Balfour were more or less in the plot is only an excuse for that virtuous indignation which is the first need of the party politician, especially at election times. The truth is far too serious for such platform trifling. The real gravamen of the story is that the British Empire should be so ill-informed as to have a vast armament built up under its nose without its knowledge, and so boyishly governed that by overreaching itself in a public-school game of bluff it should have spent ten thousand of our lives and seventy millions of our money, besides ravaging with war a whole country in which there were not one-tenth as many grievances to be remedied as there are in the parish of Lambeth, within gunshot of the doors of its Parliament. And now, since the delinquents have not the moral courage to own that it was honest ignorance and not knavish statecraft that landed us in the war, we have the usual hypocrisies of public life: the casting back to waste-paper treaties, the hunting up of witnesses against the character of the Boers (who may truly boast, with the approval of every brave Englishman, that they have lost "all save honor"), and even the absurd pretences that our countrymen in the Transvaal found life unbearable because they were not allowed to sit on juries or to have the vote. From the pro-Outlander point of view there need have been no war : Krugerism, too old-fashioned to hold the rising Boer generations, was at the end of its tether; besides, as the Transvaal was threatening to slip meanwhile under complete control by one capitalist clique or another, it is reasonable to conclude that the capitalists have been as much overreached as the Government by the unexpected development of their attempt to hurry the process by pressure from Downing Street into a war which has made the Empire, and not themselves, master of their property.

And here we see how the situation may be saved in virtue of the fact that there were better grounds for taking back the Rand than we were conscious of. Those mines belonged by law to the Government of the South African Republic; and when the working of them was conceded to private adventurers, they were taxed and regulated on that understanding. They now belong by conquest to the British Empire. The shareholders are entitled to the value of their plant and works, measured by what it would cost the Government to replace them, and not a farthing more—not even to that if we claim the spoils for the victor. If we do not retain those mines in public ownership as firmly as Lord Penrhyn holds his slate quarries, we shall have it said of us that we were neither honest enough to keep out of the money market nor clever enough to secure our gains. The elector who does not ask his candidate whether he means the Rand gold to become and to remain the public property of the South African province of the Empire is not fit to exercise the franchise.

The Settlement.

The settlement of South Africa, if it is to be an intelligent one, and not a mere suppression of popular liberties by the old Dublin Castle methods, will force us to ask ourselves what are the conditions of internal stability in a huge Empire as regards white colonists who can, if the bargain is a losing one for them, follow the example of the United States and declare their independence? It will hardly be disputed by any sane person that we cannot permanently hold Australasia, Canada, or South Africa by military force against the will of the white inhabitants. It is also clear that since we have no territorial aristocracy to train the villagers of these huge territories in reverence for the House of Lords, we must give them constitutions not only more republican in tone than that which satisfies the parish of St. James's, Piccadilly, and the peasantry of the home counties, but involving wider genuine liberties and higher practical opportunities than the American constitution, which they can adopt if they please by secession. Any power or influence over them which the British Government exercises must be exercised as a trust for the common interests, not only of the whole British Commonwealth, but of the whole of civilized society. Their incorporation must sensibly enhance their self-respect, enlarge their freedom, and confirm their security. There must be Freedom of Speech, Freedom of the Press, Freedom of Political Combination for all parties, including the party which will inevitably exist in every province, and which, for the sharper criticism of our Government, it is desirable should exist, for the advocacy of separation and independence. There must be no such crimes as Rebellion or Treason to incriminate constitutional agitators with rioters and homicides, and no practically irresponsible High Commissioners to stir up strife by University high-table talk and such question-begging terms as rebel, traitor, disloyalty, and so forth. There must be a Representative Imperial Council with a veto on war, not necessarily in permanent session in London, but available whenever and wherever required, to which the provinces of the Empire or their neighbours can appeal; so that their lives and goods shall never hang on the competence of a casual proconsul. There must be Responsible Government in the sense of Ministers holding office only so long as they enjoy the confidence of an elected legislature. If, in an emergency such as the present, the Common Law has to be set aside for the moment, and what is called Martial Law substituted, the Military Tribunal should have no judicial powers except to detain responsibly accused prisoners until, on the restoration of order, they can be released or tried under the ordinary safeguards of liberty. The least enlargement of this power makes Martial Law a specially objectionable form of Lynch Law, since officers, in the heat of warfare, easily confound justice with vengeance, and are, besides, professionally trained to regard the exercise of popular rights as mutinous.[1]

[1] The extraordinary incident of the digging up and mutilation of the dead body of the Mahdi by Lord Kitchener, significantly paralleled the other day by the desecration of the European cemetery at Pekin by the Boxers, is a sufficient example of the way in which the military mind, after a campaign in a barbarous country, loses touch with civilization.

With such constitutional rights and guarantees as these, colonists will cling to the Empire, and pioneers will invite us to annex them. Without them, every sturdy citizen of a British province over seas may at any moment cost us the expedition thither of seven of our soldiers: two for him to shoot, two to die of enteric fever, and three to wrestle with him for his gun, and to wrestle, in the long run, unsuccessfully. The simple answer to the military plan of holding the Empire by force is that it is impossible. The pretension to it only destroys the prodigious moral force which is at our disposal the moment we make inclusion in the British Empire a privilege to be earned instead of a yoke to be enforced. Our one threat should be the threat of repudiation and the withdrawal of our officials. It would be so powerful that no British province would dare, in the face of it, to abuse its powers of self-government to institute slavery or debase the standard of life for its workers. On the other hand, an invitation to fight, which is the correct description of a threat of force, would probably be accepted, unless we are to assume that the British provincial will be less sturdy than the Boers have shewn themselves.

What we have to do in South Africa, having rightly or wrongly shattered to pieces the governments of the South African Republic and the Orange Free State, is to guarantee a free constitution and responsible government within the Empire to the white inhabitants of these vast territories from the earliest moment at which it may be possible to make up the registers and summon a local Parliament (a necessary condition which will allow plenty of time for things to settle down), and in the meantime to restrict the powers of the military tribunals to committing persons for trial with the Habeas Corpus Act suspended, thereby relieving Lord Roberts from the odium of countenancing vindictive and irritating sentences on persons who, as everybody knows, will be amnestied when order is restored.

Pending the election of local Parliaments, the new provinces should be granted the following conditions:

I. Formal inclusion in the British Empire, with the privilege of using its flag.[1]

---

[1] As this matter of the flag may easily cause more irritation than more substantial matters, we may as well bear in mind that it is not necessary to enforce privi-

II. The charging of the mines and the land with a Royalty and a Land Tax to meet the expenses involved in setting up a new administration, and to make it clear that the incorporation into the Empire is a real one, and not merely an expedition to secure private property for European speculators at the public expense. At the same time, since some addle-headed persons are discussing a "war indemnity," it is necessary to remind them that a war ending in annexation of the vanquished combatant cannot also end in an indemnity. When the Transvaal and Orange State are part of ourselves, to "bleed them to the white," in Bismarck's phrase, would be to tweak our own nose. The war bill ought to be paid by an Imperial tax. As we have no Imperial taxation as yet, we must pay it as best we can.

leges. If they are real, they are soon appreciated. In the meantime, if any person wishes occasionally to wave the flag he may have fought bravely under, there is no reason why we should belittle ourselves by thwarting him. In any case, it is neither convenient nor customary for a British province to be without a distinctive flag. The Canadian Dominion and the Australasian Colonies all have their own flags, officially recognized as such by the English Government.

III. A provisional Factory and Mines Regulation Order, to secure the standard of life of the wage-earner, white or colored, in the way made plain to us by a century of experience.

IV. A Measure for the protection of the natives, to be administered by Imperial officials, not subject to local parliamentary authority.

The first three of these would be alterable by the local legislatures when elected, subject (since we have as yet no Imperial Council) to the Royal veto on legislation, which should be exercised so as to make inclusion in the British Commonwealth mean a guarantee of certain constitutional rights to all its subjects, including regulation of the relations of capital and labor so as to maintain the British standard of life as the highest in the world.

Above all, it is important that the proclamation which shall establish the new Constitution, and announce the preparation of the registers on a thoroughly democratic suffrage for the election of the local legislatures, shall be made at once. Indeed, it is greatly to be regretted that it did not form part of Lord Roberts's act of annexation. Until it is issued it will not be clear, either at home or abroad, that our

Imperialism is untainted with the lust of power over subject colonies.

ARMY REFORM.

STATES are forced at present to maintain formidable armaments, in spite of Peace Conferences, by their fear of the pugnacity and violence which are still common to civilization and barbarism. It is to be hoped that the Powers will soon have the good sense to take concerted steps to use their armaments as an international police to suppress war, on the sufficient ground that it interrupts the world's traffic, upsets its arrangements, debauches its citizens and its newspapers, and is in every way a costly and intolerable nuisance. In the meantime, it is of the most vital importance that the demand for national defence—a demand before which, in an emergency, all popular rights and liberties would go down—should not be made the excuse for imposing continental militarism upon us. We must therefore, even from the anti-militarist point of view, face the question of how to maintain an armament on the modern scale.

Shall we have Conscription?

The real objection to the continental military systems and to ours is not the violation of personal liberty implied either by conscription and compulsory enlistment, or by compulsory service after voluntary enlistment, but the demoralizing effect of barrack life and the consequent bad character and industrial inefficiency of the soldier. The commanders who now make speeches about the virtues inculcated by military service are the very men who induced us to establish the short-service system by testifying that the old soldier was a humbug. The fact that the agencies for finding employment for discharged soldiers are still very unsuccessful shews that the young soldier is no greater a favorite, except in war pictures, than the old one was. There is nothing surprising in this. The soldier is the only Englishman who is now legally a slave and an outlaw, retained in the service by force, and subject to a special form of law which sends him, without a jury, to prisons in which corporal punishment is still liberally inflicted. Stupid and careless officers thus find routine (which they mistake for discipline) maintained in time of peace for them by mere brute coercion, and go into the field without ever having had their capacity for command tested, with what result we have lately seen at Modder River, Magersfontein, Spion Kop, and other battlefields. The incompetence displayed has been so flagrant and scandalous that two generals have been sent home, a third saved from disgrace by being besieged until his blunder was forgotten, the name of a fourth blunderer hushed up, and the criticisms and confessions of Sir Redvers Buller actually published, whilst he was still in the field, for all his men to read. On the other hand, the Boers, who are not soldiers, but citizens, have astonished the world by their efficiency, and have never been at a loss for capable commanders. The obvious conclusion is that the soldier is a failure, and the militiaman, like the volunteer and policeman—that is, the fighting civilian—a success.

We suggest that the force with which England, as a modern Power, must supplant the obsolete British standing Army, which has never really got away from its origin as a pageant of royal footmen, must be created by giving to the whole male population an effective training in the use of arms, without removing them from civil life. This can be done, without conscription or barrack life, by so amending the Factory Acts as to extend the age for "half-time" employment to twenty-one, and devoting the thirty hours per week thus gained from the factory and the mine to a combination of physical exercises, technical education, education in civil citizenship (of which more hereafter), and field training in the use of modern weapons. No payment beyond a supper would be needed to make the drills popular; there would be no barrack life, and even less interference with civil life and liberty than there is in Switzerland; and we should have always available for home defence millions of men capable of dealing with a much larger force of mere soldiers.

From this force we could obtain by voluntary enlistment a picked professional force of engineers, artillery and cavalry, and as large a garrison for outlying provinces as we chose to pay for, if we made it attractive by the following reforms:

I. Full civil rights, including the abolition of compulsory celibacy and of residence in barracks when off duty on home service.

II. A "living wage," according to the current standard, for the members of the professional force as for any other public officials.

III. Service up to the age of superannuation, and then an adequate pension, with the ordinary right to leave the force at any time on giving reasonable notice, as in a municipal Fire Brigade.

IV. A salary for officers on the civil scale, with a sufficiently high standard of preliminary qualifications and daily work to make their profession a serious one.

Under such conditions there would be no need for martial law and brutal physical punishments, as there is when service is compulsory. There would be no discharged short-service men, spoiled as citizens and discarded as soldiers. Men would do much more for the service than they do now. And an incapable officer would lose his men and be found out before it was too late. Old soldiers will no doubt assure us that discipline cannot be maintained under such conditions. Sensible men will ask them how discipline is maintained in the Royal Irish Constabulary or in a municipal Police Force, in our Fire Brigades or by our railway companies, where the difficulties are as great and the dangers often much greater.

The War Office.

It is quite useless to substitute for these proposals a reform of the War Office. The War Office is simply the general business department and clearing house of the army; and in the long run every army gets the sort of business department it deserves. The Crimean War exposed the folly of our military system with sensational thoroughness. For ten years it was the fashion to abuse red tape and insist on reform. But the civilian public did not suffer; and the soldiers and officers who did had neither the political freedom nor the business capacity to agitate for and organize reform. And accordingly, fifty years later, we are again denouncing mismanagement at home and glorifying mismanagement in the field exactly as in the fifties. The truth is, the War Office as it is exactly suits the commissioned ranks of the army as it is. Both are primarily institutions for providing select positions for gentlemen, and they fulfil that purpose precisely as gentlemen like to see it fulfilled.

CHINA.

THE most obvious difficulty raised by the Chinese question has not as yet been mentioned by any English statesman. China, like Turkey, maintains a civilization which differs from European and American civilization. Without begging the question as to whether the Chinese civilization is a lower or higher one than ours, we have to face the fact that its effect is to prevent Europeans from trading in China, or from making railway and postal and telegraph routes across it for the convenience of the world in general. Now the notion that a nation has a right to do what it pleases with its own territory, without reference to the interests of the rest of the world, is no more tenable from the International Socialist point of view—that is, the point of view of the twentieth century—than the notion that a landlord has a right to do what he likes with his estate without reference to the interests of his neighbours. Nearly half a century ago we made war on China and forced her to admit our ships and give us a footing in certain ports. In concert with the Powers, we have just had to send an armed expedition to the Chinese capital to force them to tolerate the presence and the commercial and political activity of Europeans. Here we are asserting and enforcing international rights of travel and trade. But the right to trade is a very comprehensive one: it involves a right to insist upon a settled government which can keep the peace and enforce agreements. When a native government of this order is impossible, the foreign trading power must set one up. This is a common historical origin of colonies and annexations; and it may, for practical purposes, be regarded as an irresistible natural force, which will lead sooner or later to the imposition by the Powers of commercial civilization on all countries which are still refractory to it.

Unfortunately, the Powers, not excluding the British Empire, are apt to make this an excuse for purely piratical conquests of weaker States. Against this tendency it is necessary to protest. The value of a State to the world lies in the quality of its civilization, not in the magnitude of its armaments. If such an event as the annexation and assimilation of Switzerland by Russia were possible, it would be a calamity which the rest of Europe would be justified in peremptorily preventing, whereas if Switzerland were to annex Russia and liberalize her institutions, the rest of Europe would breathe more freely. There is therefore no question of the steam-rollering of little States because they are little, any more than of their maintenance in deference to romantic nationalism. The State which obstructs international civilization will have to go, be it big or little. That which advances it should be defended by all the Western Powers. Thus huge China and little Monaco may share the same fate, little Switzerland and the vast United States the same fortune.

The fate of China, however, is far from sealed. The Powers, including ourselves, have been guilty of flat piracy in China, and that, too, under the white flag of their legations instead of the black one. They tried to partition China; and it was not until they found that they were more likely to fight over the division of the spoils than to secure them that they drew back and professed the policy of the Open Door. Our attitude in the matter is perhaps best shown by the fact that we call the national movement in China to resist partition "the Boxer rebellion." It is no more a rebellion than the destruction of the Armada was.

Still, there remain our international rights of travel and trade, with the right to settled government which they involve. With these the present institutions of the Chinese Empire are incompatible; and these institutions, accordingly, must go. If the Chinese themselves cannot establish order in our sense, the Powers must establish it for them. And in undertaking our share of that establishment, we must proceed on the principle, directly opposed to that of Non-Interference, that we have international rights of travelling, trading, efficient police protection, and communication by road, rail, and telegraph in every part of the globe. Free Trade enables us to claim these rights with a better countenance than any other Power; but all the Powers claim them implicitly, and must finally do so explicitly, if only to put themselves in an intelligible moral position.

Clearly, however, these claims are reciprocal. If we have a right to go to China, the Chinaman has a right to come to us. But the huge Australasian section of the British Empire excludes Chinese, not as foreign devils, but, let us politely admit, as men so industrious, so docile, so skilful and so frugal, that they cheapen labour to a point at which the more expensive white man starves. The Australasians argue that whether the white man is worth his extra cost or not, they must not degrade his standard of life, and must therefore exclude the Chinaman under existing circumstances. Now, even if we forbear the obvious retort that the existing circumstances can and should be altered by establishing and enforcing a minimum standard of sanitation housing and remuneration for yellow and white men alike, we had better not shirk the fact that to exclude a subject of the Son of Heaven from our dominions is one thing: to exclude a subject of a Government established and guaranteed by the British, Russian, German, French, and American Powers is quite another. Clearly, if we meddle with China, and our interference does not relieve the poverty that produces emigration, we shall find ourselves in a Yellow Muddle that may bring the Chinese War into our own streets. If the Powers, to avert this danger, agree to deny to the Chinaman the international rights they force him to concede to Europe, competitive capitalistic exploitation of Chinese cheap labour on the spot will lead to a clamor in this country for protection against imports from China. On this point Imperialist statesmen must make up their minds promptly; for imports produced by foreign sweated labor have been in the past the most potent instruments of the downfall of Empires through Imperialism.[1]

---

[1] It should be hardly necessary to say here that the words Empire, Imperial, Imperialist, and so forth, are pure claptraps, used by educated people merely to avoid dictionary quibbles, and by uneducated people in ignorance of their ancient meaning. What the colonies are

Free Trade.

The decision should, as far as it rests with England, and lies between Free Trade and Import Duties, be firmly in favor of Free Trade. Socialism has demolished the Manchester School and discredited the Free Trade Utopia of its economists and dreamers; but all the king's horses and all the king's men can no more set up import duties again than Napoleon could bring back the marquises. What Socialism can do is to guide and develop export trade on the one hand, and on the other to nationalize such necessary trades as agriculture, engineering, etc., if the course of free trade threatens to take them abroad (as it might take abroad the business of national defence if we put up our military expeditions to be tendered for by competing contractors). Foreign imports cannot harm English industry as a whole: what they can do, often very beneficially, is to drive capital and labor out of one method or one trade into another.

driving at is a Commonwealth; and that is what the English citizen means, too, by the Empire, when he means anything at all.

Thus employers may be driven from the sweating-den method, which is wasteful and cruel, into the regulated factory method, which is cheaper and better, though it requires abler direction and larger capitals. Or a trade may be exterminated by the fact that it can be done better abroad than at home. It is, of course, our business to see that the superiority of the foreign product in quality or cheapness is not due to the superiority of foreign education or consular organization and activity; but when a trade is fairly beaten, and is not a necessary part of a complete communal life, its capital and labor must seek a new outlet, and should not be encouraged to sit down and cry vainly for a protective tax on consumers. Now it may prove that the qualities which have made the Chinaman so dreaded a competitor in British and American labor markets may enable him in his own country, even under the lee of a Labor Code, to maintain his health, self-respect, and industrial efficiency, and bring up his family well, on a smaller wage than the Englishman in England can. If by doing so he can exterminate the wretched trades typified in Hood's

Song of the Shirt (which is as true to-day as it was when it was written, in spite of all the cultured tears that have dropped on it), giving us the articles these simple trades produce without the misery they now cost, so much the better for us. The labor they now degrade and the capital they waste will then produce exports to pay for them; and the various English industries will compete with each other for this export trade. And as production for export depends for its success mainly on quality of product, knowledge of foreign markets, and organization of production, whilst production of cheap sweated articles for consumption on the spot demands no higher qualifications than the common East End sweater possesses, the extermination of a sweated trade by Chinese competition, and its replacement by an extension of export trade, is an advantage to be courted and not a calamity to be staved off.

"Panem et Circenses."

The real danger of adding vast and prodigiously fertile provinces to the Empire lies in our anti-socialistic system of leaving the organization of our industry, and consequently the employment of our masses, to the hazards of commercial speculation. It is impossible to forget that in the Roman Empire it proved cheaper to make Rome a parasite on the labor of the provinces, and keep the Roman proletariat quiet by providing them gratuitously with bread and circuses, than to invest capital and organize industry at home. Already our imports exceed our exports, not merely on paper through the omission of freightage, etc., from the calculation, but in reality; and the day is coming when it will be as possible for all England to live barrenly on unpaid-for imports representing rent, dividends and tribute from without, as it was for Rome, or as it is for Eastbourne at present. Hitherto the possibility has not troubled practical men, because we have not had provinces on the Roman scale. But if the industrial development of China and the Soudan placed us in possession of a Tom Tiddler's Ground, to which capital emigrated whilst labor remained unemployed at home, we should soon have to choose between "panem et circenses" and revolution, if we were still too stupid and selfish for Socialism, which, with regard to any particular industry, or to all industry, is the true alternative to Free Trade.

It may be said that the moral is not to face Socialism, but to let China alone. But how if the other Powers will not let China alone, or if China will not let us alone? The practical moral is that Empire will ruin us, as it ruined earlier civilizations, unless we recognize that unearned income, whether for British individuals living unproductively on British labor or British Islands living unproductively on foreign labor, is a cancerous growth in the body politic, and is no more necessary to commerce than it is to the public services. And we must lay the foundations of International Socialism, as we are laying the foundation of National Socialism, by making the British flag carry with it wherever it flies a factory code and a standard of life secured by a legal minimum wage (of which more presently). It is not enough for trade to follow the flag when the flag has followed irresponsible explorers who "purchase" concessions from tribal chiefs who do not know what concessions mean: civilization must follow the flag. And it is becoming more and more our concern that no flag that does not carry a reasonable standard of life with it shall be the flag of a Great Power. All our future alliances and co-operations with the other Powers for the settlement of the East, or of Africa, should be directed to this great end. It is because we have at present no social principle of this kind to guide us in our treaties that we flounder so lamentably in foreign policy as we do, and are so invariably bested by the old-fashioned dynastic imperialism of Russia, which by ruthless governmental energy and pioneering grit has taken the northern half of the continent of Asia whilst we have been shirking our manifest destiny in South Africa. We plume ourselves on being the only people that can colonize and civilize foreign provinces, as if Siberia and Algeria, Tunis and Martinique, did not exist. In truth we are the only nation that ever raised the uselessness of retaining colonies into a political doctrine.

PART II
HOME AFFAIRS

HOME AFFAIRS.

Our Home Affairs are rather a painful subject just at present. We have justified our war with the Boers on the ground that they were guilty of lèse-democracy, nepotism, and financial corruption. At the same time more than a third of our adult males (not to mention our eleven millions of adult women) are purposely disfranchised by impossible conditions of registration;[1] and the House of Commons is practically if not legally barred to all but rich men. Our entire diplomatic service, and the most influential positions in our home administrations, are openly manned by nepotism. Cabinet Ministers cannot prevent their relatives acquiring shares in companies engaged in military industries which are nursed by the Government; the House of Commons represents private commercial interests as

[1] The number of adults in the British Isles in 1898 was estimated at 21,474,391, and the number of adult males at 10,215,236. The number of registered electors (including many duplicates) was 6,528,629.

much as any Chamber of Commerce ; and the supposed alarming spread of pauper lunacy has just been at least partly accounted for by the fact that our relieving officers are bribed by asylums to bring them patients, and our doctors bribed by the relieving officers to certify the patients' insanity. The European spectator would be more than human if he spared us the obvious remark that those who live in glass houses should not throw lyddite bombs.

The Working Classes.

Accordingly, the working classes, who have deliberately chosen plutocracy for the sake of its pickings, have never been so satisfied politically as they are at present. Their masters are spending money; and they are touching their hats. Rich candidates smile whilst they are being fleeced for "subscriptions," and poor ones withdraw disheartened. Our tactful aristocracy are, as ever, pleasant-mannered and "willing to do anything for the poor except get off their backs." Our public men are only too glad to interpret Democracy as meaning that the people shall express their wishes, and the statesman, their obedient servant, shall carry them out. It is not possible to speak too contemptuously of such an attitude, in which laziness of character and laziness of intellect in governors and governed find reciprocal subservience a convenient working arrangement, and in which no political doctrine seems in touch with facts except Lord Rosebery's opinion that the popular course to take is to drop programs, win the Derby, and remind the nation, in a vein of genial expostulation, that Englishmen somehow generally muddle through all right. And so, since the working classes, with their huge voting majority, will neither help themselves politically nor even decently support the handful of labor representatives who have fought their way into Parliament in spite of them, their interests will receive little attention, and that little mostly verbal, at the election now in progress. The Minority Report of the last Royal Commission on Labour (1891-4), signed by Messrs. William Abraham, Michael Austin, James Mawdsley and Tom Mann, sets forth all that still disgraces us in our poverty, our sweating, our excessive hours of labor, our carnage in the shunting yard, our poisoning in the chemical factory, our steady wholesale manufacture of undersized Imperial Britons in slums, the shortcomings in our Factory Code, and the inadequacy of the powers of our local authorities. On these matters the Fabian Society has nothing new to say on behalf of the wage-earners as a class. Its General Election Manifesto of 1892, its Plan of Campaign for Labor of 1894, are still in print, as true, and as little regarded by the majority of those to whom they were addressed, as when they were written. We have no intention of rewriting them.

Labor Policy.

Fortunately, government cannot be quite reduced to a mere traffic in doles and votes between Ministers and people who make themselves troublesome. Our Home Policy must include a Labor Policy, whether the laborer wants it or not, directed to securing for him what, for the nation's sake, even the poorest of its subjects should have. It is clear that employers who make fortunes, not by their skill in organizing industry so as to secure the best possible supply of our needs, but by their rapacity in screwing down the share of the product given to the laborer in wages, are living on the nation's capital in the most ruinous way, besides creating ugliness and noisomeness, disease and crime, for which other people have to pay. They are parasites of the most mischievous kind, conducting parasitic industries, and sweating workers who are themselves parasitic, sometimes on relatives engaged in genuinely productive industries, but more often on the Poor Rate and on private charities. Until about ten years ago it was left to the Trade Unions to fight against this abomination. Then some of the newly constituted local authorities took up the question; established a "moral minimum" wage for unskilled labor; and pledged themselves to pay at Trade Union rates to artisans. Finally, the Government formally disclaimed competition wages for laborers, without, however, ceasing to pay them, as the Fabian Society proved in 1893. It is now admitted that competition wages are, for millions of our people, starvation wages, and that starvation wages mean national deterioration, parasitism in our industries, and fortunes made by unscrupulous and incompetent employers at the expense of their neighbors. Unfortunately, the activity of Trade Unions and local authorities covers only a corner of the vast field of labor. The time has now come for a resolute attempt to suppress sweating by the legal enforcement of

A Minimum Wage for Labor.

At present the most prosperous industries from the public point of view are those in which Trade Unionism and Factory Legislation have between them enforced a minimum wage and a maximum working day. But the electoral pressure of such formidable Trade Unionism as is possible in the cotton factory and the coal mine can only be wielded by a select and relatively small section of our wage-earners. For the millions of unskilled and half-skilled laborers, as for women and for young people, there is no real protection but the law; and the law must come to their rescue, not in response to such inarticulate and unorganized agitation as they are capable of, but because it is not good for the whole body politic that they should be neglected, overworked, and starved. The chief objection alleged against a legal minimum wage is that its enforcement is inquisitorial and impossible. This is in a sense true, just as it is true that our Income Tax is inquisitorial and impossible, and has been resisted and discredited in France and America on that ground. Nevertheless we contrive to raise a handsome revenue by Income Tax; and we should reap a much handsomer one in national soundness and reduced disease bills, crime bills, and inefficiency bills (the heaviest of the three) by a Legal Minimum Wage, in spite of all necessary exceptions and undetected evasions. As usual, the cry of impossibility comes from people who do not know that already the living wage is fixed in large industries, not by the employers dealing separately with their workmen, but by an arbitrator standing between the whole body of employers and the whole body of workmen. To make the arbitrator a public Commissioner, and enforce his awards legally, is clearly the way to begin; and the novices who imagine a Minimum Wage to be impracticable mean only that they do not know how to begin. The experience of the last six years in New Zealand under its Industrial Conciliation and Arbitration Act has proved that commercial prosperity does not depend on our method of allowing industrial disputes to right themselves by strikes and lock-outs, which, as the public hardly seems to realize, are really sieges and blockades in which more lives are lost through privation than an average South African battle costs. Victoria has for the last three years systematically fixed and successfully enforced a legal minimum wage in certain trades by Trade Boards. New South Wales is now following suit. But we go calmly on in our old lazy and wasteful way, though we have had such lessons as the upset of the Government's shipbuilding program by a lockout in the engineering trade, and the spoiling of the naval manœuvres by the Welsh coal strike.

It is not necessary here to go into the details of the measure further than to say that Trade Unions should retain their present freedom from attack through litigation, except as regards awards under the proposed law, and that no arbitration law will be workable unless based on the full legal recognition, expressed in the Act, of the Living Wage. On this basis it will not be difficult to devise the requisite administrative machinery, which will probably take the form of elected Trade Boards for different industries. Such Boards would be needed also for the piecemeal application of the General Eight Hours Act suggested in the Minority Report of the Labour Commission, already alluded to.

THE HOUSING QUESTION.

UNDER existing circumstances the supply of decent dwellings for the wage-earning class is far in defect of the demand and of the requirements of public health. A working man often has to pay his landlord simply as much as can possibly be screwed out of his wages : that is to say, much more than he can thriftily afford. Consequently, if a minimum wage were established, the slum landlord would promptly attempt, and in many cases successfully, to pocket at least a part of it in increased rent. This must be met by removing the restrictions which now prevent local authorities from providing housing accommodation. Without this any effective enforcement of the law against overcrowding is impossible.

But municipal housing, though a necessary remedy, is too slow to be sufficient. In some of the blackest spots on the poverty map of London, housing schemes have been on foot for ten years past without getting beyond the stage of paper and red tape involved by the negotiations of the Vestry, the Local Government Board, and the County Council concerning the requirements of an unworkable Act. It is easy to say that this state of things will cease *if* the house-farmers who now constitute the majorities on our Vestries are not elected (they are quite sure to be) as Borough Councillors under the new Act, and *if* the Local Government Board is reformed so that it will no longer be forced to obstruct all local activity in order to save itself from being crushed by the weight of fresh business which the recent wholesale creation of new local authorities has put upon it, and *if* a new Act is passed giving local authorities full powers to hold land and build without any restriction as to "working-class dwellings" and "unhealthy areas." Doubtless these things will have to happen; but in the meantime we shall continue to raise our local revenues by a method of rating which is, in effect, a heavy tax on houses. Imagine the effect of shifting this tax to any other necessity of life: say bread, or matches. Popular resistance would be overwhelming: the tax would have to be shifted to income.

But as we are accustomed to our rating system, we tolerate the taxation of houses, and never think of its effect on the supply.

We therefore suggest that the socialistic policy of Grants in Aid, which the anti-Socialist Liberals have opposed as a policy of Doles, can be extended to the housing industry. In the Parliament now being elected, the five years period of the Agricultural Rating Act will expire. By that time the erroneous opposition to its principle, having received no popular encouragement, will have lost countenance; but the objection to its evident favoritism towards the country landlords will remain, and will lead to a demand for extending its benefits. It will then be quite possible to provide for the payment by the Treasury of rates, or half rates, on well-built sanitary houses fulfilling such conditions as would insure that the tenants belonged to the wage-earning class, and that the rents were not higher than a fair percentage on the rateable value.[1] Such an arrangement would stimulate

---

[1] There is a precedent for this. The Inhabited House Duty is remitted on dwellings under £20 annual value, provided the local Medical Officer of Health certifies that

both municipal and private enterprise in the matter of housing ; and if its cost were met by a further graduation of the Income Tax, or by any other of the various financial expedients for recovering the unearned increment for the benefit of the community, it would be, in principle, a model measure.

they comply with the local bye-laws and are sanitary. Unfortunately there are sometimes no bye-laws of any value. "Sanitary" is a vague term; and the public body employing the Medical Officer is often manned by slum landlords. The Medical Officer's certificate, to be of any use, must give precise details as to cubic space, sanitary appliances, and the number of persons for whose use they are available, etc., in addition to the usual general terms descriptive of the condition of the premises.

MUNICIPAL TRADING.

Centuries of private trading and political corruption have left us with a strong and pernicious tradition that every public need means a job for a commercial company or a contractor. This has developed a tyranny of joint stock companies, whose directors, promoters and shareholders, not to mention the moneyed classes in search of lucrative investments, regard the modern system of Municipal Works Departments, carrying out public works at cost price to the ratepayers without the intervention of a contractor, as a monstrous invasion of the opportunities of private enterprise. This year the Government, which has shewn itself on all such questions as easily gullible as English Governments usually are, let itself be persuaded to hold an inquiry into Municipal Trading, the wires being pulled by speculators in telephones and electric lighting and traction, who, hoping to make the needs of the towns in these supplies a source of profit, found that the local authorities preferred to do the work themselves. The game of these speculators is to induce the Government to refuse powers to local authorities, and so force the citizens into dealing with private companies. Now the supply of electric power or any other commodity is to a commercial company only a means to the end of getting the largest profit and the highest interest on its capital that can be extorted from the consumer in price. A local authority, on the contrary, borrows capital from investors, or even from the central Government itself, at a lower rate than any company can borrow on the Stock Exchange. Its members cannot share any profits, and have no interest except to secure their seats by supplying their constituents as well and as cheaply as possible. The movement against Municipal Trading, though some of its spokesmen are acting in well-meaning ignorance, is at bottom a commercial intrigue to prevent the ratepayer from escaping from the claws of the companies. If any candidate at the election shews the slightest weakness on this subject, he should be voted against without regard to party. And the opportunity should be seized by the next Government to enlarge the powers of local bodies until they are able to force private enterprise into its proper sphere, which is not the exploitation of common needs and ascertained processes, but the sphere of invention, initiative, and the creation of new needs and new industries. There is an encouraging precedent for this in the action of the present Government when it was betrayed by Lord Salisbury's old-fashioned ignorance of local government, and the clamor of the financial scamps who, with their newspapers, form part of the following of all Governments, into an attempt to destroy the London County Council. When it came to the point, Lord Salisbury and Mr. Balfour very sensibly confessed that they had blundered, and changed their Bill for the demolition of the Council into an Act under which the financial scamps, hoist with their own petard, will have to deal, no longer with sleepy and incompetent Vestries, but with twenty-eight strong Borough Councils, plus the County Council established more safely than ever.

It does not follow, unfortunately, that future attempts of the same kind may not be more successful. Within the last few years the political self-satisfaction of the nation, and the insignificance of the disconcerted Opposition, have raised a new terror in English politics: the terror of retrogression. Formerly it was possible to say that in England each successive Government would begin loyally where its forerunner left off, without attempting to undo its work. Indeed, this is the true criterion of a nation's fitness for parliamentary government; for it is evident that if our parties were to spend their alternate periods of office in repealing the legislation achieved by their opponents during the previous period, we should have to find some other way of conducting the affairs of the nation. But there have been moments lately when the Government shewed signs of yielding to the corrupt pressure of purely commercial interests, and attacking our Factory Code. It took half a century of successive Factory Acts, met by successive methods of evasion, to evolve the Acts of 1847, 1850, and 1874, which defeated the sweating manufacturers by abolishing the Relay System. By far the worst mistake the present Government has made has been the introduction of a Bill under which it would have been possible to re-establish the Relay System and re-introduce factory sweating in a form with which our Factory Inspectorate could not cope. And most unfortunately this came, not as an isolated blunder, like the original draft of the London Government Act, but as the climax to an administration of the Factory Code by the Home Secretary, and a use of his large powers of government by administrative order, which had spread consternation among those who knew the gravity of the interests at stake. We suggest to the Conservative Party that it cannot afford to have reactionary Home Secretaries. It tried that expensive luxury from 1886 to 1892; and if the forthcoming elections were as dependent on Home Affairs as the 1892 election was, Sir Matthew White Ridley would probably cost his party as dear as Mr. Matthews did.

In short, then, if the electors know their own interests, there must be no debasing of the English standard of life, and there must be no attempt to suppress municipal freedom of trade. If manufacturers have not sufficient business ability to make money without sweating their employees and dodging the Factory Inspector, they must do without fortunes and find some occupation suited to the limits of their capacity. And if the English citizen chooses to supply himself with electric, pneumatic, or hydraulic power, light railways or tramways, artificial stone for municipal paving or forage for municipal horses, cottages and block dwellings, water, light and heat, with fittings and stoves, and indeed any commodity whatsoever, at cost price, with capital costing only 3 or 4 per cent. on the joint credit of himself and his fellow-ratepayers, he must not be forbidden in the interests of parliamentary joint stock directors, who boast of the millions of the capitals of their own companies, but denounce the imposing growth of municipal capital as "a huge increase of local indebtedness." We invite Ministers who feel impressed by such directorial rhetoric to glance for five minutes through a Municipal Year-Book, and consider whether they had not better be guided by the irresistible development of public enterprise they will find recorded there than by the oraculations of city gentlemen who are supposed to understand industrial politics because

—if the unmannerliness of the comparison may be excused for the sake of its exactitude—they have raced through life with their noses to the slot of the money market.

At the same time the reaction from the narrowness and sordidness of competitive private trade, and the recent exposure by the late Lord Chief Justice of its omnipresent corruption, need not carry us into a new idolatry of local authorities. It is urgently desirable that their present powers of appointing unqualified persons to municipal offices should be abolished, and the municipal services filled in the same manner as the general Civil Service. At present, in many places, nepotism and the use of municipal appointments to reward electioneering services are almost as rampant in parochial as in high Imperial affairs; and no precaution has been taken against them in the recent legislation on the subject. The new Municipal Borough Councils, for example, may, if they please, appoint as clerks men who cannot read nor write. Of course they will not go so far as that; but they will certainly fall just as short of the opposite extreme, since they can hardly be expected to surrender voluntarily their coveted powers of patronage by spontaneously adopting a system of examination and selection by independent and disinterested educational bodies.

Another important municipal question is that of the water supply. In view of the modern developments of house-to-house distribution of mechanical energy, electric, hydraulic and pneumatic, from generating centres, the need for keeping water power in public hands, and out of the hands of private syndicates (except as lessees of the public) is of vast importance. Further, the difficulties of ordinary water supply are becoming complicated by the practice of bringing water to towns from neighboring or distant counties. The water areas of the country will have to be delimited, and vested in responsible public authorities—probably the County Councils.

THE DRINK QUESTION.

It is one of the numerous paradoxes of English politics that the Question of the Drink Supply should be regarded as the special concern of the only persons who, having solved it completely for themselves, might reasonably be supposed to have least to do with it: namely, the Teetotalers. And they handle it ineffectively because they do not realize that compulsory teetotalism is as fantastically outside practical politics as compulsory vegetarianism, or compulsory churchgoing, both of which practices are very earnestly believed in by many earnest and worthy people.

The Drink Question is the question of how best to supply drink to those who want to drink, without permitting drunkenness. There is no way of having this done automatically except by making the drinkseller bear the expenses of drunkenness as well as pocket the profits of keeping a drinkshop. At present the publican (usually only a brewer's agent) takes the profits, whilst the ratepayer bears the loss, definitely in police rates and hospital rates, and indefinitely and incalculably in the inefficiency and irregularity of drink-demoralized labor. If the rate-payer kept the drinkshop, he would not make a customer drink enough to cost the rates ten shillings for the sake of making sixpence profit on the liquor account. The self-acting reform, then, is Municipalization of the Liquor Trade.

The Public House.

The public house question is a separate question. A great deal of the opposition encountered by the teetotalers is raised in defence, not of drink, but of the public house as a social institution which has its communal value in spite of its admittedly mischievous exploitation by the brewer and distiller. To many teetotalers it never seems to have occurred that sociability is so highly important a virtue that it is a point of honor with the moneyed classes to exercise it in the most extravagant fashion; so much so that it is quite safe to say that most families in fashionable and would-be fashionable circles spend more on it than they ought. And a great part of this expenditure is for intoxicating liquor. Now it is very hard to persuade people that one Englishman is like another. The man whose income is sixpence a minute will not be persuaded that the man whose income is sixpence an hour is very like himself, and depends for his social position on a cheap social machinery of treats at public houses as much as a millionaire does on a dear social machinery of dinner and shooting parties. And just as a legislative attack on the dinner parties would be unanimously resisted by the world of fashion without the least thought of the drink question, so an attempt to suppress public houses will be resisted by the huge class which has no other organ of sociability, quite apart from its opinion of temperance as a rule of conduct.

An adequate supply of public houses is therefore a necessity of the situation. The fact that the brewer, through his agent the publican, exploits the public house as a drink-shop, and multiplies it beyond all reason, is not an argument for abolishing the public house, but for municipalizing it, thus changing it from the drinkshop of a private speculator into a really public house managed by a real publican. Our present private-publicans disregard the law against serving persons who have already had as much as is good for them; and they would encourage drinking if that were necessary. It is unfortunately so far from being necessary that the publican, when he remonstrates with a drunkard at all, does so with the object of saving him from ruin and making him drink with greater sobriety, regularity, and (consequently) permanence. But in crowded districts the publican has no time for preaching; and the mere fact that at every corner we find a shop in which drink is supplied on demand, without any question of encouragement or discouragement, leads to intolerable evils. That is why the agitation for reform has overshot its mark and become an agitation for the total suppression of liquor trade and public house indiscriminately. For Local Option, though nominally stopping short of prohibition, means prohibition wherever the teetotalers have a majority. Here there is some excuse for the teetotalers themselves, because they believe that the nation would be better without intoxicating liquors, and they do not realize that no legislation can force an unconvinced nation to abstain even if such legislation could get enacted. But it is neither good sense nor good electioneering in statesmen who are not themselves teetotalers to angle for the teetotal vote by offering a measure which, on the face of it, would fortify the private drink trade impregnably in the drunken districts for the sake of suppressing it in the sober ones.

EDUCATION.

Our educational machinery in England is in a notable mess. Some places have two or three public authorities spending rates and taxes on different sorts of schools, whilst others have none at all. In one town the clever boy or girl finds in the infant school the lowest rung of an unbroken ladder to the University; whilst in the very next county there is no rescue for talented poverty from the shop or the plough. Some school districts are too small to maintain a decent primary school: others are large enough to run a University. The central organization is as chaotic as the local. At least seven separate Cabinet Ministers have schools officially under their charge; and their several departments usually scorn to consult together. The result is that although we spend on education every year nearly twenty million pounds of public money of one sort or another, we get very little for it. In English education to-day, waste and want go hand in hand.

Into the details of this disheartening muddle, and the means by which it may be reduced to order, no reader of Imperial election literature would follow us at present.[1] The subject, to the importance of which everyone pays lip-homage, is a positively repulsive one, because the nation does not believe in what it calls education, and consequently has no real interest in or patience with it. Probably not a single vote is at present turning upon it, except in a hostile direction. Its cost is thoroughly grudged; and if it were not that the breakdown of the apprenticeship system has made public technical instruction a necessity; that sectarian strife finds its battlefields in the School Board elections; and that the schoolhouse, no matter what is taught there, is clearly a safer place for city children than the gutter, it may reasonably be doubted whether the ratepayer would tolerate a twentieth part of the school rates he now submits to. The truth is that our standard education still means in England a social qualification

[1] Both are fully set forth in a Fabian Tract entitled "The Education Muddle and the Way Out," now in the press.

for the rank of gentleman. It is useless for any other purpose ; and the classical, mathematical, or philosophical knowledge which it is supposed to involve is, after all, notoriously not possessed by University graduates as a class. No wonder, then, that the Conservative citizen objects to pay for educating the masses because education does not befit their rank; the Radical objects because it is useless, except as a mark of caste; and everybody objects because his particular views in religion and politics are not inculcated—nay, are perhaps even denounced—under the head of moral instruction.

This state of things will continue, no matter how cleverly we reform our Education Department and our school authorities, until the instruction given in our schools becomes as obviously useful and helpful as food, clothing, and fresh air. At present, in certain favored districts, a poor boy who happens to be an apt scholar can, by means of our educational machinery, become a professor of University classics, University economics, University philosophy, and so forth. If every poor boy in the kingdom did the same, our system would have attained its ideal. But the country would incidentally have been ruined for want of manual workers, organizers, distributors, and public officials. We obtain these from the ranks of the unscholarly, with the result that our workers are uneducated, and our scholars uninstructed and unbusinesslike. In short, we have no education properly so called: we have only technical instruction on the one hand, and scholarship on the other. Neither our men of action nor our scholars are educated in citizenship. We have no citizens: we have only amateur politicians, with just schooling enough to make them the dupes of journalists as ignorant as themselves. Now a genuine old-fashioned Empire, autocratically, oligarchically, bureaucratically governed, can do without trained citizens; but we are not such an Empire: we are constituted as a democratic Commonwealth in which the statesman is finally at the mercy of the voter, who as yet never dreams of describing himself, or expecting anybody else to describe him, as a citizen, but is quite naturally and properly spoken of as "the man in the street."

Let us consider how this situation bears on

some of the proposals in these pages. We point out the need for a reformed Consular Service, and for a greater Indianization of our Eastern bureaucracy. But how are we to select our reformed consular staff, or our Indian officials? We have no test but the test of an education which is no education. The competitive examinations by which we obtain our upper division civil servants would be as likely as not to exclude the sort of man who would be successful in organizing British trade in a foreign market. Bengal is prolific of young natives who can commit to memory a whole volume of Mr. Herbert Spencer's Synthetic Philosophy with less effort than it costs an Englishman to learn the multiplication table; and this very docility and avidity for ready-made ideas enables them to pass examinations as effectually as it unfits them for governing men and coping with emergencies. Yet we have no better means of estimating capacity than the educational test, applied by examiners who are its own products. It is only within the last few years, and mainly on the initiative of men whose public conscience has been awakened by Socialism, that political science has at last obtained official recognition as a subject of public education. A year ago, if a County Council, Vestry, or Municipal Corporation wished to secure a clerk certificated by a University as properly instructed in statistics, taxation, and municipal constitutional law, it could not do so, nothing of the kind being available except the familiar University examination in obsolete political economy treatises compiled by professors for professors without any reference to or knowledge of the problems of practical administration. The new London University has a Faculty of Political Science which at last supplies this need; but it is only a fragment of our educational system, whereas it should be the most important part of it. The real educational problem which confronts our statesmen is not the struggle of the Church with the Nonconformists for the souls of our elementary scholars, but the establishment of quite new subjects and methods having for their object the technical training of the public servants who will constitute the executive of the Empire, and the education in citizenship of those upon whose votes their authority will be based.

The Press.

How ignorant the electorate is at present may be judged by its newspapers, those written by gentlemen for gentlemen being in many respects the worst. And there is and can be no check on the Press at present, except the knowledge and good sense of its readers. Only the other day the London papers circulated an account of the massacre of the legations at Pekin, with British officers shooting their wives to save them from dishonor, and other melodramatic particulars. In consequence, the Dean and Chapter of St. Paul's were with difficulty restrained from celebrating a funeral service for the supposed victims. The whole story, like the Pigott letters and the accounts of the heroic defence of the Jameson raiders at Krugersdorp, was a pure fabrication. A private person perpetrating such a hoax would be dealt with very severely. An Indian or Irish patriotic paper doing half as much harm by a criticism of the Government would be suppressed, and its editor imprisoned. To the London paper nothing can be done. It may be better to suffer the Freedom of the Press to be abused than to destroy it by imposing even the commonest moral obligations on it by law. All the more urgent is the need for politically educating the man in the street sufficiently to compel editors to respect his intelligence. If the State does not educate the public, the public will not be able to educate the Press; and the mutual reaction of an uneducated Press and an uneducated public is a force strong enough to dissolve an Empire.

THE MORAL OF IT ALL.

The moral of it all is that what the British Empire wants most urgently in its government is not Conservatism, not Liberalism, not Imperialism, but brains and political science. Most of our Cabinet Ministers at present are like captains of penny steamers put in command of a modern battleship. They have dropped even the pretence of competence, and bring forward dummy Bills containing a few perfunctory clauses, knowing that when the Bill goes into committee private members who have studied the subject, or who have been coached by the various interests concerned, will bring forward the necessary amendments and turn the dummy into a real Bill. This may be defended as an ultra-democratic method of legislating; but it has two disadvantages: first, that the corrupt interests are just as energetic in trying to collar the Bill as the public interests, and have much better opportunities, the Cabinet being incapable of distinguishing between them : second, that it reduces the Cabinet to the condition of the bottomless sedan chair. But for the honor and glory of the thing we might as well have no Cabinet at all. Our public men have no technique : they have been trained on bad Latin verse-making instead of on modern statesmanship. The Colonial Secretary, because he has graduated in municipal business, and understands from commercial experience how to get things done and to deal with practical men, easily overrides his colleagues, though his international manners are so bad that not even the importance of maintaining cordial relations with so near a neighbor and valuable a friend as France restrained him from making that reckless and shocking speech at Leicester, which contrasts so painfully with the letter in which Admiral Seymour has shewn how England should behave in the persons of her public men. Yet he towers, in point of practical ability, over colleagues who have not even the humiliating excuse of stupidity for their inefficiency, the truth being that though they have talent enough as Members of Parliament go, they will not work at their job. In their departments, instead of being masters of their departmental subjects, with ideas as to the solutions of the problems confronting them, they are, as the Belgians disrespectfully say of constitutional monarchs, mere "india-rubber stamps," impressing themselves at the end of documents placed before them by the permanent officials, or at most deciding, after much prompting, between two alternative official policies laid before them, the right policy being almost certainly one unsuspected by the officials, who, having never been outside their own offices, are as likely to solve the problem as a purblind millhorse might be.

The whole theory of our administration depends on the supply of political ideas and initiative from the Cabinet to the departments: without it, bureaucracy becomes an obstruction to progress instead of its most powerful engine. When the ideas are forthcoming, we get government, whether we agree with the ideas or not; and that is why Mr. Chamberlain has governed the country from the Colonial Office, whilst Mr. Chaplin has allowed the Local Government Board to become a byword for jobbery,[1] and the laughing-stock of every Town Clerk in the country. It is not the War Office and the Colonial Office that are the failures of the present Government, but the Local Government Board and the Home Office; and the cause of it is not any personal corruption or stupidity or ill-will on the part of Mr. Chaplin and Sir Matthew White Ridley, but simply that they do not understand their work, and, having taken no pains to improve themselves in this respect, have been at the mercy of the manufacturers whose interest it is to slip off the yoke of the Home Secretary, and the company promoters and building speculators to whom inefficient local government secures monopoly and large profits. Besides Mr. Chamberlain, the only Minister who has stood

---

[1] As the public have lately connected jobbery mainly with contracts, it had better be explained here that the precise accusation implied in the above sentence is that of giving away the appointments which are practically in the gift of the President of the L. G. B. as rewards for electioneering services to the Minister's party in his own constituency. It is astonishing how few English gentlemen have sufficient public intelligence to understand that this is a grave political misdemeanor.

like a rock for his own policy is Mr. Walter Long, the Minister of Agriculture; and that policy has been, not the energetic reorganization of agriculture exemplified for him by Denmark, by our own Colonies, and even by Mr. Horace Plunkett in Ireland, but—the muzzling of dogs!

All through our bureaucratic system we are hampered by the separation of the secretarial from the executive officers : in India, between Simla and the man actually building the bridge or governing the province; in the Local Government Board, between the clerks at Whitehall and the masters of workhouses, Town Clerks, and Borough Surveyors; in the Home Office, between the officials and the governors of prisons, inspectors of factories, etc.; in the Education Department, between the men who have never had an hour's experience of teaching and the schoolmasters; in the War Office and Admiralty, between the clerks, bound hand and foot with red tape, and the officers on service. The climax of all these separate sources of friction is the universal friction between the Treasury and every other human institution, official or otherwise.

Whatever else the war may do or undo, it at least turns its fierce searchlights on official, administrative, and military perfunctoriness. Before the war, we were secretly proud of the frowns of Europe, because we thought we were hated for our superiority. Europe is now smiling, which is not quite so easy to bear. German officers give us good-natured hints about our cavalry and our formations. Russian diplomatists look forward with confidence to settling the Chinese question with a British High Commissioner of the calibre of the gentleman who at Bloemfontein explained the superiority of English institutions and the excellence of English intentions to President Kruger in the manner of a British governess talking to an Egyptian fellah. We have made military reputations for Cronje and De Wet, and left many of our own laurels on the field. The Government very greatly deceives itself if it believes that these things have filled the nation with a sense of glory. The brief days of window-breaking and hat-blocking, exhilarating to ourselves, but unspeakably ridiculous to the European spectator, have passed; and we are now asking ourselves, as a Government journal has just rudely put it, " Are we a Nation of Fools ? " The reply is that we are probably not more foolish than other nations, but that we are intellectually much lazier. We cling to our aristocracy ; and our aristocracy is ready to die for its country, but not to live for it ; to do any quantity of tedious duty under orders, but not to earn the right to be intrusted with that duty by learning and thinking about it. Politically we have no standard either of intelligence or capacity: the responsibilities of the age of Great Powers have found us a nation of cricketers governed by a bench of golf players, ready to " shift the enemy with the bayonet " (an obsolete weapon, our officers tell us), but not to shift the impersonal enemies of civilization with the providence of high statesmanship.

It may be that nothing will rouse us but some staggering calamity or some unbearable humiliation. Not until civil war was organized did we reform our Parliament in 1832. It took two cholera epidemics to force us into Public Health legislation, and a Crimean War to reform our Civil Service. Yet these reforms were as nothing compared with the reforms that lie before us—and immediately before us, if we are to hold our own in the modern international movement.

Our purpose here, however, is not to call idly on the Government or the nation to "make an effort." We know well that the effort we desire can only be made by men who have our ideas and our faith in our ideas. If we were Conservatives or Liberals ourselves, we, too, should be lazy, cynical, indifferent, ignorant, sceptical as to the value of measures which would be to us aimless. By placing our ideas at the disposal of the Liberal Party, and adapting them to its use by enlarging the Nottingham Program to the Newcastle one, we only precipitated its present ruin. We frankly say now that the Conservative Party will fall into the same confusion by meddling with the measures we propose, and trying to unsocialize them by throwing the cost of them on some scapegoat class instead of on the whole community, as it has already thrown the cost of national insurance against accidents on the employers. The confusion will last until conscious Socialism creates a party with a purpose and a faith; and then English statesmen will once more have a craft and master it. We have never affected a humble estimate as to the future of Socialism in England. Long before Mr. John Morley made the discovery, we said plainly enough that when the exhaustion of Liberal ideas led to the disappearance of Liberal leadership (which is precisely what has now happened), Liberalism would be supplanted in its representation of progressive ideas by Socialism. "You must either follow the Socialists," says Mr. Morley, in effect, "or follow me; and I have no particular destination to lead you to." Mr. Chamberlain, still brisk enough to start out on the chance of turning up somewhere, has already compelled the Conservatives to follow him by forcing the same alternative on them. He, too, will presently find that there is only one way forward. That way is our way: the way of International Socialism. We are quite aware that our countrymen will not believe us. We can only say that as soon as they find an alternative we shall be ready to discuss it: meanwhile, Nature abhors a vacuum, and will fill it with Socialism because nothing else is available.

THE END.

CHISWICK PRESS: CHARLES WHITTINGHAM AND CO.
TOOKS COURT, CHANCERY LANE, LONDON.

Printed in Great Britain
by Amazon